GRANITE CHIEF WILDERNESS

Barker Pass

WARD PEAK

MTWIN PEAKS

Alpine Meadows Ski Area

BARKER PEAK

SCOTT PEAK

STANFORD ROCK

Tahoe Rim Trail

Ellis Lake

Paige Meadows

ELLIS PEAK

Barker Pass Rd

Lake Loise

Quail Lake

OHV Trail

Homewood Mountain Resort

89

EAGLE ROCK

Blackwood Cyn Rd

Sno-Park

Ward Creek State Park

Granlibakken Resort

To Truckee

89

To Tahoe City

Tahoe Pines KASPIAN RECREATION AREA

Sunnyside

Homewood

Creek ground

Chambers Landing

To Incline village

28

TAHOMA ♡ of the west Shore

Pine Point Park

HOE'S MAGICAL WEST SHORE

North →

LAKE TAHOE

S0-AVB-859

Tahoe's
MAGICAL WEST SHORE

Jill Beede

A Tahoe Country Guidebook/Keepsake

Tahoe's Magical West Shore
Copyright © 2001 by Jill Beede
All rights reserved

Published by:
Tahoe Country
P. O. Box 13186
South Lake Tahoe,
CA 96151-3186
Phone: 530-544-6600
Fax: 530-544-2411
www.tahoecountry.com

Book design by Jill Beede
Cover collage and map design by
Betty Barsamian
Cover illustrations: see page 203
Edited by Mike Stuckey
Printed in Canada

Publisher's Cataloging-in-Publication
(Provided by Quality Books, Inc.)

Beede, Jill.
    Tahoe's magical west shore : a
Tahoe country guidebook/keepsake /
Jill Beede. -- 1st ed.
        p. cm.
        Includes bibliographical refer-
        ences and index.
        ISBN: 1-931476-01-2

        1. Tahoe, Lake (Calif. and Nev.)--
    Guidebooks.
    I. Title

F868.T2B44 2001   917.94'3804'54
                            QBI01-200308

For those who live here,
frequent our shores,
or have yet to come.

CONTENTS

INTRODUCTION

Welcome to the Magical West Shore, the stretch of Lake Tahoe from Tahoe City to Emerald Bay that enchants regular visitors to return year after year and draws new ones under its spell each day. In this guidebook, longtime local writer Jill Beede explores the Tahoe of granite and centuries-old cedars, cobalt-blue bays, wilderness areas, wildflower-covered meadows, and snow-capped peaks—sharing stories of yesteryear while giving practical information of interest to trip planners and locals alike. This is the Tahoe where lodgings range from lakeshore campsites to quaint cottages, cozy knotty-pine A-frames to grandiose lakefront estates. Meals range from simple sandwiches at one of the local deli counters to elegant four-course dinners at lakeshore restaurants, some even offering valet boat parking. Summer or winter, this is the Tahoe where how much recreation you can pursue on any given day is limited only by how much sleep you need. Throw a dart at a map of the West Shore and anywhere it lands won't be far from fishing, hiking, skiing, snowboarding, camping, boating, rock climbing, in-line skating, sledding, snow-mobiling, water skiing, parasailing, ice-skating, mountain biking, four-wheeling and a host of other activities. This is the Tahoe where museums and historical displays let you explore man's impact on the area, from the earliest Native American visitors to the loggers and resort operators who followed. It's the Tahoe where the great outdoors and wildlife are right outside the door, the Tahoe that has never grown beyond little hamlets dotting the shore. Finally, it's the Tahoe where locals remain awed by the beauty that surrounds them and take great pride in living on *Tahoe's Magical West Shore*. This guidebook is the ideal companion for a first trip to the lake or a 50th. Enjoy!

Introduction by Mike Stuckey

—The West Shore viewed from Eagle Rock. Author.

TAHOE CITY SOUTH

- Truckee River Outlet
- Dot-So-La-Lee
- The Washoe
- Gatekeeper's Cabin Museum
- Indian Basket Museum
- 64 Acres Park
- Tahoe Rim Trail
- Tahoe Tavern
- S. S. Tahoe
- Lake Tahoe Ski Club
- Tahoe Power Boat Club
- Rascals in Paradise

- Tahoe Tree Company
- Granlibakken Resort

TRUCKEE RIVER OUTLET

We begin our journey of the West Shore at the wye in Tahoe City, where Highway 28 forks off Highway 89 and heads for Nevada. Stay on Highway 89 and head south, direction Emerald Bay. You'll cross the Truckee River at Fanny Bridge, named after what you see of the tourists who often line the sidewalk on the lake side to ogle the monster rainbow trout awaiting handouts. After a heavy winter, when the lake is at its legal limit, the release of water makes it difficult to view the fish, but it's great for taking a self-guided rafting tour down to the entrance of Alpine Meadows at River Ranch. You can bring your own raft or rent one from the local concession. At the northern bank of the Truckee River Outlet, Dat-So-La-Lee, the Washoe Indians' most famous basketweaver, would sit with her front door open, weaving the legends of the Washoe people into beautiful, intricate creations.

—*Aerial view of Lake Tahoe's outlet. Ann Riordan.*

DAT-SO-LA-LEE

The Indian woman's given name was Debuda, meaning "the quiet one," but her weaving name, Dat-So-La-Lee, was derived from a lifelong friendship with Dr. S. L. Lee, the first white man to take an interest in her work. Another admirer was Abe Cohn, who began selling her work in 1895 at his Emporium in Carson City and summer curio shops at the lake. Appreciation for Indian art grew during the early 1920s, and the superior skill evident in Dat-So-La-Lee's baskets commanded four-digit prices, though she received little compensation for her work. Notes maintained on the 120 woven pieces Cohn acquired were all prefixed with the initials L.K., denoting Luisa Keyser, the name Dat-So-La-Lee took when she married Charley Keyser. It is also said that she hated the name Dat-So-La-Lee, which meant "wide of Hip" and prefered to be called by her English name.

—*Dat-So-La-Lee. Nevada State Museum.*

14

THE WASHOE

Washoe Indians from Carson Valley were the first to enjoy Lake Tahoe's shores. Forced from the lush California valleys perhaps as long as 4,000 years ago, this small band of Native Americans developed a pattern of migration to exploit resources at different times of the year. In spring, the Washoe came to Lake Tahoe: da ow a ga ("giver of life," as they called it). Locations for their summer encampments were chosen for the abundant quantity of foods and medicinal plants. During their encampment, the Washoe gathered supplies for the winter. Women gathered willow, redbud and fern root to create the Washoe's most important tool—baskets. Today, they are valuable pieces of fine art admired by all, but for the Washoe, these intricate containers were used for cooking, eating, carrying water, and collecting seeds and plant materials.
—*Indian Women at the Outlet of Lake Tahoe, California. Circa 1912. Author's collection.*

2521 – INDIAN WOMEN AT OUTLET OF LAKE TAHOE, CALIFORNIA

GATEKEEPER'S CABIN MUSEUM

The Gatekeeper's Cabin Museum, situated among ancient conifers on the south bank of the outlet, was built in 1981 with funds raised by the North Lake Tahoe Historical Society. Built by Art Thiede in the Canadian scribing method, the hand-carved log cabin is built from lodgepole pines. It stands on the same foundation as the original Gatekeeper's Cabin, which was destroyed by fire in 1978. The museum features the history of Lake Tahoe, including Indian artifacts, natural history displays, stories of our pioneers, a book and photographic library, and Lake Tahoe's vintage newspapers. The North Lake Tahoe Historical Society was founded in 1969 by a group of locals who were dismayed at the many landmark structures torn down in the 1960s to build condominium developments. Lakeshore picnicking is available.

—*Gatekeeper's Cabin and the Marion Steinbach Indian Basket museums. Author.*

MARION STEINBACH INDIAN BASKET MUSEUM

Marion Steinbach's lifelong interest in Native American art and culture led her to study and collect representative baskets and artifacts. By the time of her death in 1991, she had gathered over 1,000 rare and diverse baskets, dolls and artifacts, each of which she carefully described and documented—truly a world-class collection. Marion was herself a weaver of considerable skill and artistry, and taught basket-weaving classes each summer at the museum. It was her intent to collect a variety of basket and artifact types from as many tribes as possible, and the woven works range in size from burden baskets measuring nearly three feet in diameter to highly detailed sample pieces as small as one-quarter inch. The museum's Eva Buck Gallery features exceptional baskets and pottery.

—*Interior of the Marion Steinbach Indian Basket Museum. Deby Zwierlein-Carter.*

TAHOE TAVERN, 1901-1960

Just south of the museums, on what is now Tahoe Tavern Properties, once sat the Tahoe Tavern, one of the world's finest destination resorts. It was designed by famous architect Walter D. Bliss for Duane L. Bliss—the Comstock lumber giant who at one time owned three-fourths of the lakeshore. When the tree supply diminished, Bliss turned to tourism. The Tavern featured such amenities as a barber shop, bowling alley, ballroom, theater, pleasure pier, laundry, resident physician, stables, golf links, a swimming pool, an automobile garage (converted into an indoor skating rink during the winter), a self-contained water system and steam plant. The toboggan hill, which was reached by teams of horse drawn sleighs, is now part of Granlibakken Resort.

—*Tahoe Tavern. De Macrae collection.*

Tahoe Tavern
in Winter

Tahoe Tavern guests included such Hollywood luminaries as Will Rogers, Nelson Eddy, Charles Laughton and Bing Crosby. The steep rates for a stay were deemed reasonable by the upscale clientele in light of the extravagant hospitality. Guests were originally transported to the Tahoe City area from Truckee's main depot by six-horse stage, but a narrow gauge railway was constructed by Bliss's Lake Tahoe Railway and Transportation Company in 1899 to cover the 16-mile run from Truckee to a trestle pier one-eighth mile long that was built in front of the tavern. The hotel enjoyed tremendous popularity and prestige until 1960 when ballooning expenses, age, and changing visitor tastes forced its sale to real estate developers. In September 1964, a horde of fans snapped up the tavern's furnishings at a gala public auction, and demolition of the famous hostelry soon followed.

—*Dancing at the tavern. De Macrae collection.*

S. S. TAHOE, 1896-1940

Steamer Tahoe was the most luxurious boat to roam Lake Tahoe's waters, measuring 169 feet long and nearly 18 feet wide, with two 600-horsepower steam engines. Every morning, she would meet the Truckee train at Tahoe Tavern. She then began her eight-hour journey counterclockwise around the lake, delivering mail, baggage and other cargo. She could hold 200 passengers in the 100-foot-long elegant deckhouse on her topside—decorated with teak, mahogany and cedar paneling, polished brass, imported carpeting, crimson plush fabric and Moroccan leather. White marble lavatories had hot and cold running water. The 30-seat dining room below the decks served extravagant meals prepared aboard. She served Tahoe for close to 40 years, until the expense of operation sidelined her in 1934. In 1940, she was scuttled near the Bliss home in Glenbrook.
—*The Steamer Tahoe. Don and Jeanne Davis collection.*

3071 – Steamer Tahoe, Lake Tahoe, California.

64 ACRES PARK

Just down from the museum lies 64 Acres Park, with a raft launch on the Truckee River, allowing a descent down to River Ranch (leave a second car there). Hikers and bikers have a choice of many backcountry destinations reachable from the west side of the park: Tahoe Rim Trail, Granite Chief, the Pacific Crest Trail (no bikes allowed), Paige Meadows and Stanford Rock (popular with mountain bikers). Many of these trails are used in winter for cross-country skiing and snowshoeing. The park has ample parking and is also a good place to join the bike trail for a ride down the West Shore, to Squaw Valley, or to Dollar Point. The land was given to the U.S. Forest Service by the U.S. Bureau of Reclamation for public use. Plans now are to locate a transit station and interpretive center in the park. At the lake side of the park, there is a nice sled hill and a small public beach with picnic tables.

—*The Truckee River. Artist Melinda Plumbridge.*

TAHOE RIM TRAIL (TRT)

The Tahoe Rim Trail is a 150-mile, twenty-four inch, single-track trail open to hiking, equestrians and mountain biking. The trail encompasses the ridge tops of the Lake Tahoe Basin, crossing six counties and two states. Two trailheads exist on the West Shore: one at 64 Acres Park and another at Barker Pass. Mountain biking is allowed everywhere along the West Shore portion except on the Pacific Crest Trail. Camping is allowed on all portions of the trail. A wilderness permit is required to enter areas located within Desolation Wilderness. The 13-mile portion of the trail between the two West Shore trailheads zig-zags from glorious views along the Sierra crest, through canyons brilliant with wildflowers, to the cool forested rim of Lake Tahoe. At the head of Ward Canyon, a small seasonal waterfall drops into a sparkling pool creating an excellent spot for photos or a picnic.

—*Meadow along the trail. Tahoe Rim Trail Association.*

LAKE TAHOE SKI CLUB

In 1926, after the Bliss family sold the Tahoe Tavern and their former chef, Jack Matthews, took over as manager, the tavern opened for short winter seasons. They built an indoor ice rink using the parking garage and constructed a toboggan slide and a world-class ski jump "trajectory," reached by horse-drawn sleigh, on what is now Granlibakken Resort property. In 1929, Matthews called for the forming a ski club, in order for the tavern's winter sport facilities to be awarded the site of the USSA Ski Jumping Championships for the 1932 Olympics. The idea met with great enthusiasm and the Lake Tahoe Ski Club was formed. These first "Nationals" to be held west of the Rockies drew record crowds. After the tavern discontinued its winter operation in 1936, the club moved to several different locations before eventually calling Squaw Valley its home. —*Ski jumping. De Macrae collection.*

Ski Jumping at Lake Tahoe

TAHOE POWER BOAT CLUB

In the early teens of the 1900s, wealthy vacationers to Lake Tahoe succumbed to their curiosity as to whose motorboat was the fastest by holding informal races sponsored by the Tahoe Tavern. These primitive boats screamed along at a mere 20 mph, but early marine pioneers held their victories in high esteem. In 1925, the Tahoe Power Boat Club was formed and the grand era of racing began, only to end at the onset of World War II. Later, in the early 1950s, the traditional "locals-only" format was replaced by national races and the Tahoe Yacht Club no longer featured Lake Championship races. Instead, the club began exhibitions of unlimited boats and separate competitions for dragboat hulls and stock runabouts over 25 feet. Today, the club is best known for its annual Concours d'Elegance during Wooden Boat Week in August.

—*Art from the 1992 Concours d'Elegance poster. Artist Roy E. Dryer III.*

RASCALS IN PARADISE

Few scenes capture the spirit of Lake Tahoe's past more than
Rascals in Paradise, a recently formed wooden boat club cel-
ebrating the more traditional boating activities of yesteryear at
an annual gathering on the placid waters fronting Tahoe Tavern Properties.
Camp Rascal, as the club calls the gathering, spreads over a period of three
weeks (mid-July to early August) and includes a Domino Tournament, an
Over-the-Bottom Regatta, the "Unpredictable Regatta", and a variety of din-
ner/dances at lakeshore restaurants. Some of Tahoe's finest woodies can be
seen cruising from one lovely lakeside home to another for receptions and
refreshments, passengers and drivers dressed in "Camp" costume (circa
1940). Most of the proceeds of the Rascals' annual affair benefit the North
Lake Tahoe Historical Society.
—*The vessel "Stacey Lynn" and guests. Steve Lapkin.*

TAHOE TREE COMPANY

The grand log building on the corner of Highway 89 and Granlibakken Road has become an icon on Lake Tahoe's West Shore. Built by the Tahoe Tree Company, this structure is a good example of modern log architecture, which houses wonderful gifts and gardening hardware. High ceilings and skylights give the building lots of light even during the winter months. A leisurely stroll through the extensive nursery grounds can be a full lesson in high-altitude gardening where trees, shrubs and perennials are tastefully displayed in gardens through the nursery. If you are interested in perennials, the Tahoe Tree Company grows over 250 varieties! Periodic talks on the subject of gardening and nature crafts are held at the nursery, and from late spring to early fall, several musical events take place in the gazebo area.

—*A popular variety of lupine. Evelyn Nored.*

GRANLIBAKKEN RESORT

At the end of Granlibakken Road (off Highway 89) sits the largest year-round resort on Lake Tahoe's West Shore. Though primarily a conference center, there are facilities available for use by all. The small historic ski hill (see Lake Tahoe Ski Club) offers two runs and is the site of a torchlight parade on Christmas Eve. At the base of the mountain, there is an old-style warming hut with a snack bar and a popular sled hill nearby. You can start at Granlibakken for a pleasant seven-mile (mostly intermediate level) cross-country ski trek. A popular way to begin is at the top of the poma lift, then continuing uphill for one mile to Lookout Point for a magnificent view of Lake Tahoe. From there, you can continue a couple of miles to Paige Meadows and return via the same route, or by a steeper descent ending on the fire road just east of the resort.
—*The West Shore viewed from Talmont. Ann Riordan.*

SUNNYSIDE TO TAHOE PINES

- Paige Meadows
- The Showy Red Snowplant
- Sunnyside Hamlet and Resort
- Alpine Meadows Ski Area
- Telemarking and Backcountry Skiing
- Stanford Rock Loop
- Biking Ward Canyon/TRT/to Truckee River
- Kaspian Recreation Area
- Blackwood Canyon Area
- Middle and North Fork OHV
- Barker Pass
- Pacific Crest Trail

- Ellis Peak Trailhead
- Granite Chief Wilderness
- Eagle Rock
- Legend of Eagle Rock
- Idlewild
- Fleur du Lac

PAIGE MEADOWS

To get to Paige Meadows, continue south along Highway 89 from Tahoe City. Turn right on Pine Street, the third street past Corpus Christi Catholic Church. Take the first right, Tahoe Park Heights Drive. At the crest of the hill, you will come to an intersection. Take the middle fork. The road then turns into Big Pine Road. Follow this road out to Silvertip, turn left, and park at the end of the road. After a short descent through a scenic forest (about 10 minutes), take a path off to the right, which will lead you into the first of five expansive flat meadows—great for cross-country skiing, mountain biking, walking, and picnicking. In late spring, there are fabulous wildflower displays. Make sure you bring mosquito spray. It is easy to miss the turn into the meadows from the main trail, so you may wish to have a topo map and compass with you.
—*Fall in Paige Meadows. Ann Riordan.*

THE SHOWY RED SNOWPLANT

A curious site in the Tahoe landscape as the snow melts is the bright red snowplant (Sarcodes snaguinea), a member of the wintergreen family. This strange asparagus-like plant does not photo-synthesize, but receives its nourishment from parasitizing the roots of neighboring plants and other decaying organic matter. It is protected by California law and there are heavy fines for tampering with the snowplant due to its extreme beauty and rarity (it is found only in the yellow pine and red fir forests of California and southern Oregon). Other common wild-flowers in the area include: BLUE/PURPLE lupine, dwarf aster, meadow penstemon; PINK/RED indian paintbrush, shooting star, columbine; YEL-LOW/ORANGE mule ears, buttercup; WHITE corn lily, cow parsnip, ranger buttons, common yarrow, and mariposa lily.
—*Snowplants. Author.*

SUNNYSIDE – HAMLET AND RESORT

Sunnyside, the most commercial of the West Shore's communities, has a couple of markets, the William Kent Campground and Beach, a realtor, bike rental shop, a couple of restaurants, power boat, jet ski and sailboat rentals, a marina and opportunities to fish for Tahoe's big lake trout. Sunnyside Resort is a popular spot to have a drink and/or dine year-round. In winter, they keep two roaring fires going and monitors in the corners to watch skiing and snowboarding. On Wednesdays in the winter, crowds begin arriving around 5 p.m. for the 2-for-1 fish tacos. The resort offers a shuttle service to the back entrance of Alpine Meadows ski area most weekends—buy your ticket aboard. The deck opens in spring, generally with a live music party around Mother's Day and becomes a favorite spot to dine and watch sunsets and the speedboats coming in and out of the marina.

—*Sunnyside Resort. Douglas Byrne.*

ALPINE MEADOWS SKI AREA

One of the most popular ski resorts in the area, Alpine Meadows offers a world-class mountain, and has one of the longest seasons—generally closing at the end of May. It boasts 2,000 acres, a vertical descent of 1,802 feet and more than 100 runs, the longest being 2.5 miles. Views from the mountain include a view of all of Lake Tahoe from the summit. Though the main entrance is located off Highway 89 between Tahoe City and Truckee, there is lift access (the Sherwood Chair) off the West Shore. To utilize it, you must either hold a season pass or buy tickets from Sunnyside or Granlibakken Resort, and have your equipment. There is a shuttle from Sunnyside Resort most weekends and you can buy a ticket aboard. There is no parking at this entrance, but you can drop someone off there (Highway 89 to Ward/to Courcheval).

—*Telemarking with Hirsch. Courtesy Ralph Silverman.*

TELEMARKING AND BACKCOUNTRY SKIING

Alpine Meadows is a favorite mountain for those who have taken to telemarking, which has had a significant revival in the area during recent years. This old-style skiing is easily recognized by the graceful telemark turn—obtainable from the lack of a heel attachment. Many feel that telemarking offers the same thrills as regular Alpine skiing, without the discomfort of its cumbersome equipment. In addition to regular alpine skiing and snowboarding clinics, Alpine Meadows offers telemark lessons and is host to several telemark events each year. Off the groomed slopes, telemarkers have many other places along the West Shore to practice their turns. Some hike West Shore mountain peaks on snowshoes or by putting skins on their skis. Others roam the many hundreds of miles of ungroomed trails along the West Shore on their scale-bottomed all-terrain skis.

—*Twin Peaks. Ann Riordan.*

STANFORD ROCK LOOP

Mountain bikers have a choice of several different loops, of all levels, departing from either the William Kent Campground across from Sunnyside Resort, or by driving to the Ward Creek area. Off Highway 89 just south of Sunnyside, turn right on Pineland, left on Twin Peaks Road—which turns into Ward Creek Boulevard. Park one mile up the road near the junction. The turnout on the left leads up to the summit of Stanford Rock and ties into the Tahoe Rim Trail coming down from Twin Peaks. This popular 11-mile loop comes out back into Ward Canyon and gives longer ride options to Paige Meadows and Scott Peak. It is a technical trail (stone staircases and massive water bars) with an elevation gain of 2800 feet. On the way up, there are great views of Lake Tahoe and Barker Pass, and from the top of Stanford Rock you can see Twin Peaks, Sherwood Forest and Scott Peak.

—*Twin Peaks. Tahoe Rim Trail Association.*

BIKING WARD CANYON/TRT/TRUCKEE RIVER

A more moderate loop (10 miles) begins farther up Ward than the Stanford Rock Loop. After Ward Creek Road changes to Courchevel, turn right on Chamonix and park where 16N48 goes off to the right—where you will begin your ride. From 16N48, take a right at the next Y intersection, then bear left onto the Tahoe Rim Trail (TRT) at the west end of Paige Meadows. Follow the TRT to the Truckee River at 64 Acres Park, then go south along the bike path back to Pineland and up Ward Canyon. This section of the Tahoe Rim Trail is a fun, windy, roller coaster ride through forested areas with a great descent ending at the river.

—*Bike trail along the Truckee River. Tahoe City Public Utility District.*

KASPIAN RECREATION AREA

At the entrance to Blackwood Canyon and Barker Pass is the Kaspian Recreation Area. Though the beach is quite pebbly and located right along the roadside, it is a popular spot to do shore fishing, swim or just watch the boats pass by. There are picnic tables, barbeques, a restroom and 10 camping spots. In winter, this is a California "Sno-Park" site. Kaspian is an interesting place to see some of Lake Tahoe's strange weather effects too. Predicting the weather in Lake Tahoe is a difficult task, especially in the winter. As storms are located off the coast, it's hard to predict how they will act once they hit shore. Sometimes they loom over the Sacramento Valley and break up before they hit the Sierra, or, if it isn't cold enough the Tahoe Basin receives *Sierra Cement* (wet snowfall). Then the East Wind might arrive and freeze everything solid.

—*Just north of Kaspian Recreation Area. Danielle Hansen.*

BLACKWOOD CANYON AREA

A popular gateway to the high country is just across from Kaspian Recreation Area. The first few miles (on Blackwood Canyon Road) are smooth, straight and fairly level, which makes it popular with in-line skaters and bike riders. At 2.5 miles, the road veers left to head up to Barker Pass. If you continue straight onto the dirt road, you arrive at the off-road staging area where there are picnic tables, barbeques and bathrooms available. Just before the staging area, off to the right, there is a practice shooting range. Free rustic camping is available in the area, but limited to three days. In the winter, the area is popular with snow shoers and cross-country skiers. The road closes at the beginning, in winter, and you must buy a parking permit if you park in the California Sno-Park at its entrance. Snowmobilers need OHV green stickers.

—*Blackwood Canyon area. Ann Riordan.*

MIDDLE AND NORTH FORK OHV TRAILS

Mountain bikes, dirt bikes, jeeps and ATVs have a choice of moderate to level trails from the staging area.

Middle Fork (2.5 miles): Continue past the staging area. Veer left onto 15N38. There are some steep areas and creek crossings, but the trail is not rocky. At 7,000 feet there is a meadow that fills with wildflowers. The trail ends near the base of Barker Peak, and from the upper flats there are spectacular views of the area.

North Fork (3.5 miles): As above, except veer right at the fork onto15N41. The beginning mile is difficult on dirt bikes and mountain bikes due to lots of loose rocks. Farther up, there are tricky creek crossings, small steep banks, followed by good views, then it dead ends.

—*The Official Greeter at Lake Tahoe. Author's collection.*

35588

BARKER PASS – GATEWAY TO THE WILDERNESS

At 2.5 miles from the highway, instead of going straight onto the dirt road to the staging area, veer left and continue on the paved road that crosses Blackwood Creek and then begins a rather steep seven-mile climb to Barker Pass. You can park in the first lot at the top and hike up to Ellis Peak. A half-mile farther, at the Pacific Crest Trail trailhead, is a larger lot with a toilet—used as a staging area for hikers and horse pack trips, though cars and trailers may not remain overnight. This is a good jumping-off point for mountain bikers of all skill levels, although they are not allowed on the Pacific Crest Trail. Beginners will have a blast exploring the logging roads that crisscross the area, and more advanced riders can head southwest and join the Rubicon jeep trail.

—*One of the many views from Barker Pass. Dick Singer.*

PACIFIC CREST TRAIL (PCT)

The Pacific Crest Trail, perhaps the most beautiful of America's scenic trails, spans 2,650 miles from Mexico to Canada, and is easily accessed from the West Shore. One popular day journey is to ride horseback from Barker Pass to Bayview at Emerald Bay (only hiking and horseback are allowed on the trail). The ride is 24 miles. The first portion from Barker is a gentle scenic route and allows for an early lunch stop at Richardson Lake. From there, the trail passes through a heavily timbered section, then, after Middle Velma Lake, it becomes the solid granite landscape that Desolation Wilderness is known for. There, you leave the Pacific Crest Trail and drop down 2,150 feet with a zillion switchbacks—but with fabulous views of Emerald Bay, Granite and Cascade Lakes. The trail season in this area is generally June through September.
—*Richardson Lake. Justin Beede.*

ELLIS PEAK TRAILHEAD FROM BARKER PASS

Where the pavement ends at the top of Barker Pass Road, the Ellis Peak Trailhead is off to the left. Parking is available. Many feel the workout to reach this peak well worth the effort for the exquisite views on top, where you can see Desolation Wilderness to the south, Hellhole Wilderness to the west, Granite Chief Wilderness to the north and Lake Tahoe to the east. The trail is popular with hikers, dirt bikers and mountain bikers. The eight-mile round-trip ride takes you along the ridge for 1.5 miles, through meadows and forests. Ellis Peak was named after Jock Ellis, who had a dairy ranch in the area. He sold dairy products to those passing by from Georgetown to the lake (on what is now the McKinney-Rubicon Trail). He had a difficult time getting cream to rise during the colder seasons, slowing his production. Eventually, he abandoned his dairy and switched to raising sheep.
—*Sunset from Ellis Peak Trail. Ann Riordan.*

GRANITE CHIEF WILDERNESS

This 25,700 acre hiking/horseback riding wilderness area is generally less crowded than Desolation. It can be reached from the top of Barker Pass by heading west on the Powderhorn Trail, or by following the Pacific Crest Trail north to Five Lakes. The latter offers some stunning vistas along the way. The southern section of Granite Chief is forested with mixed conifer, red fir and lodgepole pine in the higher elevations, and deciduous and evergreen woodlands lower down. Elevations range from 5,000 to 9,000 feet. Due to snow, this area is inaccessible before late May/early June and after snowfall begins in the fall. Camping permits are not required, but fire permits are. It is prohibited to camp within 600 feet of any lake in Granite Chief. Due to fawning season, dogs are not allowed in certain areas of the wilderness from mid-May through mid-June.
—*One of the Five Lakes. Ann Riordan.*

EAGLE ROCK

Just south of Kaspian, on the opposite side of the highway, is Eagle Rock—a great place for picture-taking, picnics and to watch sunsets. The path begins at the south side (or north side), and continues around to the back, along narrow paths of mules ear, dogwood, thimbleberry, manzanita and aspen. Then, it crosses the massive volcanic protrusion that can easily become a game of hopping and balance. At the lookout point, you'll discover all the wonders of Lake Tahoe. As you learn of Tahoe's history, it's easy to envision the shoreline of the late 1800s, stripped of its timber, with logs crossing the lake by boat— headed for the gold and silver mines of Virginia City. The great environmentalist John Muir tried to get Tahoe designated a National Park, but the decision-makers lacked his foresight.

—*Looking north from Homewood (Eagle Rock in the foreground.) Ann Riordan*

LEGEND OF EAGLE ROCK

Big Eagle, a Washoe chief, summered at Lake Tahoe, setting up his teepee at the sloping backside of Eagle Rock. In the early morning, he used to lay at the cliff's edge to hunt for deer heading to the lake for water. His bow and arrow ready, he would wait for the rustling sound in the brush below and shoot as soon as the deer came out from among the trees. His wife, Gentle Doe, would catch fish at the lakeside for breakfast. One early June dawn, Big Eagle shot at a blurred shadow coming out of the bushes. Then he heard an agonizing scream. Letting out a despairing cry, he slid frantically down the jagged side of the rock, where he found his wife lying breathless below. For many moons after, his tribesmen would see a great feathered shape perched on the edge of Eagle Rock at dawn letting out a wild cry, then it would drift away over the treetops.

—*Eagle Valley sentinel. Artist Mona Schulte.*

ILDLEWILD

The area just below Eagle Rock's bluff used to be called Idlewild, the name popularized in the 1880s for the exclusive residential section of the West Shore by Mrs. Edwin B. Crocker, the high society's acknowledged leader. For nearly 20 years, the reknowned summer "whirl" was organized by the Crockers' daughter, Aimeé Crocker Ashe Gillig Gourand Miskinoff (Princess Alexander Galitzine). She was the perfect choice to set the pace for this pinnacle of society activity, considered herself to be a worldly adventuress due to her collection of husbands. Aimeé's zesty life in the gay '90s at Idlewild found its way into her eyebrow-raising book, *I'd Do It Again*, published several decades later. The Crocker home was bought by the Kohl family in 1905, then the Fleishhackers in 1926, who expanded the property, which was later subdivided by the Everets Mills. Idlewild officially became Tahoe Pines in 1912.

—*Idlewild. North Lake Tahoe Historical Society*

FLEUR DU LAC

Fleur du Lac, a walled compound of multimillion-dollar condominiums on the lake side of the highway in Tahoe Pines
served as one of the locations for "The Godfather, Part II." The
original 16-acre retreat was built in 1935 by Henry Kaiser. Others, who
had determined this site unbuildable because of its situation in a swampy
lowland, were unaware of Kaiser's reputation for accomplishing the impos-
sible. Zillions of dumptruck loads of fill were brought in—a main lodge,
five outlying cottages, a caretaker's residence and a four-slip boathouse with
rocked-in harbor were finished and furnished in a mere 28 days! Kaiser
went about boating with the same vigor, which influenced the nature of
boating competitions at Lake Tahoe, and eventually made his name as familiar in boating circles as it was in international board rooms.
—*Kaiser Estate. North Lake Tahoe Historical Society.*

HOMEWOOD AREA

- Homewood – the Hamlet
- Jake Obexer – Marine Pioneer
- Homewood Mountain Resort
- Black Bears in the Tahoe Basin
- Stories of Bear Encounters
- Chambers Landing
- John McKinney
- David Chambers
- Rubicon-McKinney OHV
- Noonchester Mine Trail
- Buck Lake Trail
- Bear Lake Trail
- Rubicon Springs
- Sierra Club's Ludlow Hut
- Historic Log Lodge
- 1960 Winter Olympics

81

HOMEWOOD – THE HAMLET

Once a popular resort and the first stop of the S. S. Tahoe as it left Tahoe Tavern to circle around the lake, Homewood Resort provided accommodations for all tastes and wallet sizes: hotel rooms, cottages, and tents—especially popular for the gently sloping bathing beach, open-air dancing, boating and campfire activities. Today, the original Homewood Resort is gone but not forgotten, and the hamlet is populated with a combination of part-time and full-time residents who often disagree on its future growth: those who insist that some growth is necessary for the local economy, and others who prefer to keep it the "way it was." Nevertheless, Homewood offers visitors a popular ski area, boating activities, two marinas, several restaurants, a hardware store and nursery, a grocery store, a variety of lodging choices for visitors and Independence Day fireworks (July 5).

—*Homewood. Artist Paul Bartmettler.*

JAKE OBEXER, TAHOE MARINE PIONEER

Jake Obexer was a guiding force in the development of speedboating on Lake Tahoe. With the use of internal combustion engines, the lake needed a gasoline supplier, and Obexer was the only one willing to risk the dangerous transport of marine fuel. First contracting with Union 76, Jake later switched to Standard Oil (the former would not carry locals' IOUs through the winter). Obexer's–Homewood already comprised a boat harbor, marine service station and grocery store. Then, in 1931, Jake became a dealer for the popular Gar Wood speedboat. During the filming of Rose Marie (with Jeanette MacDonald and Nelson Eddy) in 1935, he was the personal marine chauffeur for its director, William Van Dyke. He was thanked with a copy of Van Dyke's next film's script—a major disappointment—until he discovered a $5,000 check inside!

—*Obexer's–Homewood. Courtesy Sarah Obexer.*

HOMEWOOD MOUNTAIN RESORT

This hidden treasure offers 1,260 acres of wind-sheltered downhill skiing and snowboarding with excellent groomed runs. Often, Homewood is the last resort in the basin to close for "wind hold." Popular for its powder skiing, Homewood is even better known for its spectacular lake views and warm hospitality. Homewood is served by eight lifts and boasts 57 runs. Many special events take place throughout the season, such as the "Locals' Triathlon" and "Pro Patrol Race" during Snowfest and the "Furniture Race," the last day of the season. Facilities include Homewood Children's Center, rental shops, ski school, two day lodges and restaurants. There are two entrances to the resort, one at the north on the highway, and another farther south (follow signs to Tahoe Ski Bowl Way). A shuttle runs regularly between the two.

—One of the many views from Homewood's slopes. Author.

BLACK BEARS IN THE TAHOE BASIN

Barker Pass was the destination point for the caravan formed to transplant black bears in the early 1940s from Yosemite, where they had become a nuisance (and still are). But that particular year, snowfall arrived early and they were not able to reach the top of Barker Pass to release them into Desolation Wilderness and they wandered down into the West Shore neighborhoods. Admired for their high endurance and adaptive nature, black bears live a slow-paced life, thriving in the High Sierra wilderness and urban fringe. While seemingly tolerant of humans, when bears meet them in their path, they either ignore them or do a bluff charge. They can be unpredictable and must be given an escape route if encountered—make noise and back away. *A fed bear is a dead bear* and locals know that by feeding them they would quickly become a nuisance.

—*A neighborhood bear. Scott Brunn.*

STORIES OF BEAR ENCOUNTERS

Bear stories are a favorite topic of conversation along the West Shore. One popular story took place in the late 1940s. A San Franciscan named Arthur came to the lake for the first time with three friends who had a cabin in Homewood. On the journey over the mountain, they told Arthur lots of bear stories. By the time they reached the cabin it was dark. They asked Arthur to go outside to fetch some wood but as soon as he heard rustling in the bushes he came running back inside. Arthur's friends suggested he camp out back in the little cabin since there was no food there to attract the bears. Then they maliciously made noises outside Arthur's cabin to scare him. When the prank was done, they returned joyfully to the kitchen—where they found the largest black bear they had ever seen.

—*Meeks Bay bear. Courtesy Don and Jeanne Davis.*

THE HUT AND BEN CALLENDER

As with many early pioneers, Ben Callender came to Tahoe in
1906, hoping its reknowned curative climate would help his
severe case of asthma. All it took was one summer to hook him
on the area, and the following year he returned with his brother, Howard,
to start a commercial fishing venture, planned to supply all the finest tables
in San Francisco. His canopied steamer, Lady of the Lake, served as a fishing boat and taxi. In 1917, commercial fishing became prohibited, but that
helped spur the birth of tourism. Ben opened Callender's Camp Franklin,
with a roadside retreat called the Hut, which served the best hamburgers at
the lake and was a popular stop for Tahoe City crowds heading to Meeks
Bay to dance in the 1930-40s. In 1947, he sold the Hut to retire, but later
returned to purchase his competitor's El Campo Lodge, which he ran until
his final retirement.
—*The Hut. De Macrae collection.*

THE HUT
LAKE TAHOE

CHAMBERS LANDING

Chambers Landing opens Memorial Day weekend with great fanfare at the bar on the dock (the oldest bar at Lake Tahoe), marking the beginning of summer and the boating season. Locals and part-time residents walk over to share a Chambers Punch with friends not seen through the winter. Others arrive in classic wooden runabouts and fancy racing boats for a drink or an elegant meal at the fine restaurant. From then on, the beach fills with sun-seekers, grand weddings take place with newlyweds departing by watercraft, kids have crawdad fishing contests, and all the activity ends at the end of September. The facilities, which include a pool and tennis courts (not open to the public), are owned by the Chamberlands Beach and Mountain Club, available to owners of the million-dollar lakefront condominiums and single-family homes in the Chamberlands tract.

—*Chambers Landing. Artist Bill Clausen.*

JOHN MCKINNEY

John McKinney, a pioneer wearing beaded Indian moccasins
and fringed buckskins, settled at Lake Tahoe in 1862. The
next year, he established Hunter's Retreat, catering to Nevada's
mining nabobs, advertising the best hunting and fishing at the lake. By
1869, he had a boathouse, 20 cabins and numerous tents. He offered more
rugged outdoor accommodations for free, as well as use of boats and fishing tackle. McKinney's was popularized by its lack of pretentiousness and
reputation for social equality. Visitors enjoyed listening to Old John's tall
tales and he became a living legend. In 1892, McKinney lost his resort to a
Sacramento alcohol supplier over a $600 whiskey bill. He died shortly
thereafter—a broken-spirited man. Eventually, the resort was taken over
by David Chambers, from whom the resort received its current name.
—*McKinney's. Don and Jeanne Davis collection.*

McKinney's. Lake Tahoe. Cal.   Putnam & Valentine Photo. Los Angeles Cal.

DAVID CHAMBERS

David Chambers, a hotelier from Santa Barbara, bought McKinney's in 1925, allowing him to spend his summers at Tahoe indulging in his passion for things nautical. He was a charter member of the Tahoe Yacht Club, and many a regatta departed from the Chambers pier. In 1897, the old Glenbrook House had been transported across the lake and set on new foundations at McKinney's. Chambers Lodge, as it was now called, still advertised an informal setting with hunting, fishing and loafing. Under his ownership, many of the resort's cottages were modernized, but the hotel and clubhouse maintained their reputation as an old-fashioned mountain resort. Chambers is best remembered as a kind, familiar figure with cane, cigar and bulldog, but he also served the community as fire chief and enjoyed nothing more than jumping into his bright red fire engine.

—*Chambers Resort circa 1945. Author's collection.*

CHAMBERS LODGE, LAKE TAHOE, CALIF.

MCKINNEY-RUBICON OHV ACCESS

Just south of Chambers is the turnoff to one of the most demanding 4X4 trails in America—used as a testing ground for Chrysler's Jeep. It is also the site of the annual Jeepers' Jamboree the last weekend of July and first weekend of August. From the highway, turn on McKinney Creek Road and follow the signs to Miller Lake. The first couple of miles of the trail are paved and limited rustic campsites are available along the way (campfire permit required). The beginning of the dirt trail isn't too difficult, but after you cross the Sierra crest and begin heading down toward Rubicon Springs, boulders and other obstacles line the route. The entire trail continues 22 miles to Georgetown. You can also mountain-bike, hike or cross-country ski to several lakes from the trail. Fishing is fair at Miller, Richardson and Buck lakes.

—*Looking north across McKinney-Rubicon area from Sourdough Hill. Justin Beede.*

NOONCHESTER MINE TRAIL

About 0.7 miles up the McKinney-Rubicon Trail is a turn-off to the right marked "Single lane road not maintained for passenger car use." This trail first crosses a bridge, then leads up to Noonchester Mine (2.5 miles). The views are superb looking down on Quail Lake, the Homewood Mountain Resort ski area and Lake Tahoe. The trail on the other side of the turnabout is private property. If you continue, the trail heads to Ellis Peak and Barker Pass. If desired, you can take this ride to Ellis Peak, then return to McKinney via Buck Lake—or visa versa. Mountain bikes, Jeeps, dirt bikes and OHVs are allowed on the trail. Hikers often meet bears on this trail. If you have a dog with you, make sure it doesn't charge at the bears. Then, just stare at the bears until they realize you are not threatening. They will just continue on their way. Give them room.
—*Quail Lake. Artist Melinda Plumbridge.*

BUCK LAKE TRAIL

Two miles from where the dirt trail begins up the McKinney -
Rubicon Trail, turn right onto FS road 14N40 toward Buck
Lake (it's marked). The first 1.2 miles of the road climb 900
feet through several rocky sections, so be prepared to push your bike at
times. Buck Lake sits in a narrow basin surrounded by steep cliffs. The lake
offers a pleasant picnic spot and good fishing. You can continue up the trail
and head southwest back to McKinney Road, arriving just west of Miller
Lake. Head east, passing Miller Lakes, Lily Lake and McKinney Lake to
arrive back at your point of departure. Or, from Buck Lake, you can continue on to Ellis Peak and even Barker Pass if desired. But make sure you
have a topo map with you.
—*Lily Lake. Author.*

BEAR LAKE TRAIL

To get to Bear Lake, go up the McKinney-Rubicon Trail, passing McKinney Lake, Lily Lake and both Miller Lakes. Remember, you need a good OHV for this one, or at least a high-clearance 4X4. The road to Bear Lake is marked and turns off to the right after the first Miller Lake, direction Barker Pass. The first mile is a good surface and climbs up to a ridge. Then it heads back down and circles Bear Lake. As you can see on the picture at the right, it is easy to launch a canoe into Bear Lake. There are a few rustic campsites available. You can continue on 2.5 miles to Barker Pass from Bear Lake. If you don't have a good OHV, it's easier to drive to Bear Lake from Barker Pass and back (in a 4WD). It's also easier to reach Miller Creek Road this way than directly up McKinney-Rubicon.

—*Bear Lake canoe launch. Justin Beede.*

RUBICON SPRINGS

John and George Hunsucker, miners from Kelsey, settled in the Rubicon Springs region in 1867. They built a hand-hewn log cabin and by 1880 had developed a popular hunting resort. They began bottling the spring water, but found it difficult to supply the demand. In 1886, Vade Clark bought the resort, turning it into a favorite destination spot for Nevada's health seekers, and later, wealthy San Franciscans. Her resort had 16 guest rooms with lace-curtained windows, horsehair furniture and a foot-pedal organ in the parlor. She often prepared meals for as many as 100 guests—serving them on tables dressed with white linen and polished silverware. In 1908, Vade left, and it began losing its appeal. Many others tried to manage the resort, but it was eventually sold to the Pacific Gas & Electric Co. in 1930.

—*A "one of a kind" photo of Rubicon Springs. North Lake Tahoe Historical Society.*

SIERRA CLUB'S LUDLOW HUT

Located near Richardson Lake, off the Rubicon-McKinney trail —at the northern edge of Desolation Wilderness—the Ludlow Hut offers serious cross-country skiers refuge, and eases the transition between day and overnight trips. All visitors agree, "The silence that can envelop the woods around Ludlow is almost spiritual" and the effort to ski in with a pack is well-rewarded. Accommodations are hostel style with a ladder leading to the loft, where large sections of the floor swing upward and hook into place to let the warm air circulate. Two heavy wooden tables and a pair of wood stoves dominate the lower, concrete floor. (Take your down booties!) The hut, built in 1955, was named after Bill Ludlow, a wilderness skiing enthusiast who died at age 23 in the Korean War.

—*The Ludlow Hut. Brooks Austin.*

HISTORIC LOG LODGE

This historic lodgepole pine cabin's exterior was a backdrop town building in the 1930s film *Rose Marie*, with Jeanette MacDonald and Nelson Eddy. The interior was used as the mountain cabin where James Stewart was arrested. Surrounding property became a studio encampment platform for tents and a dance floor with local bands providing entertainment for the filmmakers. In the 1960 Olympics, the property was leased for bleachers and was the turn-around point for the cross-country ski events. The current owner has a great passion for restoring historic buildings and procured the cabin in 1986, when it was a basic shell, with dirt floors and no windows. Today, it is a magnificient example of Old Tahoe architecture, with a kings truss cathedral ceiling, slate fireplace, and is decorated with period antiques. Log Lodge is available for vacation rentals (see directory).

—*Log Lodge. Ron Patterson.*

1960 WINTER OLYMPICS

Many people know that the 1960 Winter Olympics were held in Squaw Valley, but few know that the cross-country skiing events were held on the West Shore. With early abundant snowfall and rolling terrain, it is ideally suited for cross-country skiing. Olympic ski trails were narrow, single-lane with two parallel ski tracks meandering along land contours and slipping through narrow corridors carved through the forest. For seven days during the two-week Olympiad, skiers on heavy wooden cross-country skis glided through the backwoods. Race courses varied in length from 5 to 50 kilometers. There are currently efforts to reopen these trails, which will allow skiers to go from Homewood to Sugar Pine Point State Park (see directory).

—*1960 U.S. Olympic Cross-Country Ski Team. Bill Briner.*

TAHOMA TO MEEKS BAY

- Tahoma
- Aimee Semple McPherson
- The Sugar Pine
- Sugar Pine Point State Park
- Phipps Cabin
- Ehrman Mansion
- Tahoe Maritime Museum
- Lighthouse and Nature Trail
- General Creek
- Special Park Programs
- Magulu Watah
- Early Meeks Bay
- Meeks Bay Resort
- Meeks Bay Today

- Desolation Wilderness
- Fishing Desolation Lakes

TAHOMA – HEART OF THE WEST SHORE

The small hamlet of Tahoma boasts many of the amenities of a small town, along with easy access to the natural beauty and activites that draw people to the great outdoors. For visitors, it offers a nice variety of accommodations—from lakefront estates to old Tahoe-style cabins, cozy B&Bs to a year-round campground—all walking distance to a grocery store, laundromat, post office and several restaurants. In summer, the Marie Sluchak Community Park is the site of outdoor church services, free Saturday night movies, and in early December, the Christmas gala announces the beginning of winter. Once an area with few year-round residents, Tahoma has developed into a desirable community with sky-rocketing real estate prices. The town received its name from the Tahoma Resort, whose main building now houses the local grocery store.

—*A popular local band, the Roemers, playing in the park. Ann Riordan.*

AIMEE SEMPLE MCPHERSON

Well-known Four Square Gospel (Angelus Temple) evange-
list, Aimee Semple McPherson, spent time in Tahoma in the
1920s. Dressed in flowing white robes, she used the forest as a
cathedral for her popular revival meetings. Though most admitted she had
a magnetic appeal, many locals complained that there was sufficient reli-
gion in the waters, mountains and skies of Tahoe without a McPherson
type of ambassador to preach it. In 1927, she obtained 60 lots in what is
now the Tahoe Cedars tract, to be used as a summer campground for her
disciples to attend Gospel Camp. That July, hundreds flocked to the grand
opening which featured a 39-piece band. After Aimee's infamous kidnap-
ping (where she was suspected to have been shacked up with a married
man in Carmel), financial backers for the Tahoe settlement project with-
drew.
—*Tahoma Resort. North Lake Tahoe Historical Society.*

THE SUGAR PINE

"In sun-days, the sugar pine preaches the grandeur of the mountains like an apostle without moving a leaf," wrote John Muir in *Mountains of California*. The sugar pine was considered by Muir to be the most beautiful of all California conifers. Native Americans used the sugary resin as glue and savored the flavor. The sugar pine is the world's tallest pine, growing up to 175 feet high and 18 feet around. They live to be 500 years and older, do not begin cone production until the age of 150, and are capable of producing up to 100 cones per year. Sugar pine cones average one foot long and can weigh up to 4 pounds. During the logging heyday, 1863 to 1877, the two West Shore logging camps at Ward Creek and Sugar Pine Point removed 23,000 board feet per day of the precious pines.

—*Sugar Pine Point. Artist Miriam Biro.*

Sugar Pine Point

Miriam Lino

SUGAR PINE POINT STATE PARK

Sugar Pine Point State Park comprises over 2,000 acres of conifer forest in the General Creek drainage. The waters of General Creek are among the clearest flowing into Lake Tahoe and the stream is open to fishing from mid-July to mid-September. A 175-site campground is open year-round, with hot showers available in the summer months. Many miles of hiking trails and a swimming beach provide visitors with a variety of relaxing summer activities. The Nature Center displays several species of birds, most of the mammals and the four major game fish that live in the Tahoe Basin. Winter visitors will find over 20 kilometers of marked cross-country ski trails and a heated restroom in the General Creek campground. A portion of these trails was used during the 1960 Winter Olympics cross-country ski events.

—*Grounds below the Ehrman Mansion. Author.*

PHIPPS CABIN

In 1860, General William Phipps staked out a 160-acre homestead on Sugar Pine Point and became the first recorded permanent resident of Lake Tahoe's southwest shore. He arrived at Lake Tahoe with guns, knives, a bedroll, buckskins and $200 in gold dust. He was an expert marksman who hunted and fished the heavily timbered back country of lakes and canyons. He also netted silver and cutthroat trout in the stream he had laid claim to. Phipps used his rifle to fend off loggers who were stripping the basin of its timber and managed to protect his own property's giant sugar pines, but could do little to protect the surrounding areas. Phipps died in 1887, leaving his name to General Creek, Phipps Lake, Phipps Pass and Phipps Peak (the 9,300-foot mountain 1.5 miles south of Rubicon Peak).
—*Phipps Cabin. Pat Davi.*

EHRMAN MANSION

Pine Lodge was the name used for the summer home of the Hellman-Ehrman family. It set the standard for West Shore elegance. Isaias Hellman, a wealthy San Francisco banker, had acquired title to over 1,000 acres of land surrounding the mouth of General Creek and in 1904 retained the Tahoe Tavern's architect, Walter Danforth Bliss, to design his new residence. In view of the estate's isolation, the compound had its own dairy and vegetable garden. During the family's annual two-month stay, they were attended by over 30 servants, including caretakers, chauffeurs, maids, cooks, laundry workers, groundskeepers, gardeners, tailors and boatmen. Housing for these employees alone accounted for at least half a dozen buildings on the property. During the summer months, tours of the mansion and grounds are conducted several times daily.

—*Ehrman Mansion. Author.*

TAHOE MARITIME MUSEUM

The Ehrman family's two boathouses attest to their enthusiasm for marine activities. Among their mahogany-planked water toys was Ester's Belle Isle speedboat, the 26-foot brass-trimmed Cherokee. Charles Ehrman's plaything, the Jacqueline, was raced during the summer season of 1937, taking first place in the 200-plus horsepower event in the Tavern Regatta that season. The building next to the north boathouse now houses the Tahoe Maritime Museum, a non-profit organization whose purpose is to stimulate interest, increase knowledge and maintain water craft and marine artifacts significant in Lake Tahoe's maritime history. Their annual Maritime History Day, usually held on a Saturday in mid-July, features many dryland displays.

—Edna and Herb Obexer in seat, J. P. Obexer in back. Courtesy Sarah Obexer.

LIGHTHOUSE AND NATURE TRAIL

To the north side of the Nature Center is a bridge that crosses General Creek, then goes up a short hill. At the top of the hill, if you continue straight, you will be on the Nature Trail—an interpretive trail noting Washoe history, flora and fauna. This trail ends up on Highway 89 across from the entrance to General Creek Campground. If you turn right at the top of the hill, you will end up at the beach and following it north will take you to the lighthouse at Sugar Pine Point (seasonal operating). Up the ridge from the beach is a trail that heads north. This is a loop trail that joins the Nature Trail. These are well-marked, and though ungroomed in winter, are popular for cross-country skiing.

—*Sugar Pine Point lighthouse. Author.*

133

GENERAL CREEK

On the otherside of the highway is the park's General Creek Campground—the only year-round campground at Lake Tahoe. There are 175 sites, showers and a trailer refuse dump available (except during winter). Campsites are nice and large and located in forested areas. At the end of the campground loop (near site #150) is a dirt road that narrows and leads around Olympic Meadows— called such because nordic ski events took place there during the 1960 Winter Olympics. The meadows are great to view spring flowers and fall colors. This loop is mostly flat, nice for bike-riding, walking or cross-country skiing. In winter, the closed campground areas are groomed for cross-country and skate skiing, but the dirt trails are ungroomed. At the end of the General Creek loop, there are options to continue to Lost Lake, Duck Lake and Lily Pond. Leashed dogs are OK in the campground, but not on trails.

—*General Creek. Artist Paul Bartmettler.*

SPECIAL PARK PROGRAMS

In the winter, between January and March, Sugar Pine Point State Park offers a variety of free programs, just about every other Saturday. They generally leave from the parking lot at General Creek campground. Offered are several different levels of cross-country skiing, beginning snowshoeing, equipment care, avalanche safety, moonlight ski tours and animals in winter. In summer, on Living History Day at the Ehrman Mansion, park personnel dress in vintage attire and it's easy to imagine just how lucky the Ehrman family was to have this particular residence. Take a moment and sit in a wicker chair on the porch to glance down over the lawns (often covered with Canada geese), past the giant sugar pines to the lake. If you hit the right moment, you may get a chance to further your imagination if you see some classic wooden boats come in to the pier.

—*Living History Day at the Ehrman Mansion. Author.*

MAGULU WATAH (Meeks Bay)

The bay we now call Meeks Bay was known to the Washoe tribe as magulu watah. For thousands of years, this bay was one of their favored summer encampments at da ow a ga—the sacred lake in the sky, whose name meant "the giver of life". Here, fishing was good, and wild berries, currants and rhubarb were plentiful. Native grass seeds, camas, wild onions and lilies—also important in the Washoe diet, were abundant. By the 1860s, white men began harvesting hay from the meadow (Meeks & Company), followed by extensive logging (Carson & Tahoe Lumber & Fluming Co., owned by the Bliss family), and a dairy operation (the Murphy brothers). All these activities eventually interrupted the traditional summer migration of the Washoe to magulu watah, and they moved their encampment west into the hills.

—*Meeks Bay. North Lake Tahoe Historical Society.*

LAKE TAHOE, MEEKS BAY, CALIFORNIA

EARLY MEEKS BAY

While the Murphy brothers owned the property at Meeks Bay, they were spending the bulk of their time managing McKinney's Resort. The dairy farm was run by the Lunemans, but was eventually shut down for health reasons. After Vade Clark left Rubicon Springs, she contacted the Murphys about leasing property to start a resort on the bay. Much of Vade's former clientele followed her to the new location, which she had set up similarly to Rubicon Springs, with tent cabins and a common dining hall. Vade's tenure at Meeks Bay lasted a mere three seasons, as she returned to "revitalize" her family's resort at Phillip's Station. In 1921, George and Marjorie Kehlet convinced the caretaker, Martin Lowe, to allow them to camp along the bay in hopes of curing George's poor health. He was so enamored with the place that he contacted the Murphy brothers about buying lakefront property.

—*Meeks Bay. North Lake Tahoe Historical Society.*

MEEKS BAY RESORT

The Kehlets arrived with a caravan in 1922 to open their camp-ground for its first season. For 47 years, the Kehlet family ran the resort, which gained fame as one of the most popular family resorts at the lake, with dancing to live music, a restaurant, theater and marina. In 1969, the family was forced to make the difficult decision to sell, when hooking up to a sewer became mandated and cost to the resort would have been around $500,000. A corporation from Texas bought the land, with grandiose ideas of developing a virtual city of condominiums. But the parent company went bankrupt, so computer pioneer Bill Hewlett bought the land "to keep it in public hands" until the Forest Service could afford to buy it, which happened in 1975. The Forest Service concessioned the resort operation to longtime resort guests Duke and Bev Hubbard who ran it until 1997.

—*Meeks Bay Resort. Don and Jeanne Davis collection.*

MEEKS BAY RESORT
LAKE TAHOE CALIFORNIA

MEEKS BAY TODAY

In a historic move during the Lake Tahoe Presidential Forum in 1997, President Clinton signed an executive order giving the Washoe Tribe access to its ancestral lands by signing a 20-year agreement for them to utilize the Meeks Bay Meadow for the gathering of native plants. That same year, the Washoe Tribe won the bid to become concessionaire of the resort with a 20 year lease under a special use permit from the Forest Service. The resort today consists of a nice sandy beach, campground, marina, store and snack bar, and 21 cabins. The Kehlet Mansion, which sits on the point at the north end of the bay, is rented to large groups. On the south side of the creek from the resort is Meeks Bay Campground (40 units) and beach operated by a USFS concessionaire and California Land Management. The hamlet offers a grocery store, an off-road vehicle concessionaire and an import store.

—*Meeks Bay Resort beach. Pat Davi.*

DESOLATION WILDERNESS

In 1969, through an act of Congress, 63,475 acres of subalpine forests, granite peaks and glacially formed valleys and lakes became protected for visitors to experience the wilderness in a place unchanged by humans. No motorized or mechanized equipment is allowed, so travel is limited to foot or horseback. For day use, permits are available at the Meeks Bay access, but overnight permits must be obtained through the Forest Service office in South Lake Tahoe. Due to its popularity, quota systems and a small fee have become necessary for overnight use year-round. Strict wilderness ethics apply— leave no trace! Nature on its own terms includes hazards such as sudden stormy weather, high-water stream crossings and even natural fires, so visitors should be well-prepared for their trip to the back country.

—*Desolation Wilderness. Don and Jeanne Davis collection.*

DESOLATION VALLEY, LAKE TAHOE, CAL.

FISHING DESOLATION LAKES

The Tahoe-Yosemite Trail leaves Meeks Bay for Yosemite and is a well-developed major Sierra route. At about 4.6 miles in there is a series of lakes that provide fine fishing. This part of the Desolation is known for browns, and Crag Lake has some fish that move for minnow imitations. The lakes are sometimes called the Pater Noster Lakes after the rosary whose beads also form a chain. In this case, the lakes were formed by glaciers moving up and down the canyon and depositing glacial debris as they receded—something like prehistoric bulldozers. Stony Ridge Lake was the first lake planted in the Tahoe area and was the source of the Lake Trout that now inhabit Tahoe itself. At the top of Phipps Pass is Phipps Lake which is known for excellent brookie fishing. This is primarily an overnight camping area because of the distance to the first lake.

—*Crag Lake brown. Jerry Yesavage.*

RUBICON TO EMERALD BAY

- Rubicon Bay and Peak
- D.L. Bliss State Park
- Rubicon Trail
- Emerald Bay State Park
- Vikingsholm
- Fannette Island
- Boat Camp
- Underwater Park
- The Hermit of Emerald Bay
- Eagle Falls, Lake and Point
- Bayview Campground and Trailhead

- Fishing Desolation from Emerald Bay

RUBICON BAY AND PEAK

One of the most beautiful bays along the West Shore, Rubicon is today a highly desirable community of expensive homes along the lakeshore and others dotted on the hillside overlooking the bay. This is also the starting point for hard core backcountry skiers and snowboarders to reach Rubicon Peak. To get there, turn up Scenic Drive (from the highway) and continue to the top of the hill. It's not always easy to find a "legal" parking spot in winter, but if you can, take plenty of snacks and water, along with a topo map or the Desolation Wilderness map. It is a straight two-hour climb to reach this peak but well worth it for the view of Lake Tahoe and Desolation Wilderness. The descent offers some of the best tree skiing found in the Tahoe Basin. This is an especially popular spot after the local ski resort closes, but definitely for advanced-level backcountry skiers and snowboarders only.

—*Rubicon Peak. Ann Riordan.*

D. L. BLISS STATE PARK

One of Lake Tahoe's finest beaches is found at D. L. Bliss. Get there early on summer days because the beach parking lot fills quickly. The park is named after the pioneering lumberman, railroad owner, banker and Tahoe Tavern owner, Duane L. Bliss. His family donated 744 acres to the State Park System in 1929. There are 168 individual campsites available, as well as a group campground, open in summer only. On summer evenings, rangers set a bonfire for all to enjoy at the campfire center and a variety of programs is offered for the kids at the park. Rubicon Point is one of the favorite diving spots of Lake Tahoe, but it has also been the site of many diving and boating accidents. Drowning victims of Lake Tahoe's icy waters do not generally surface. This is also the site of another lighthouse.

—*Moonrise at D. L. Bliss State Park beach. Ann Riordan.*

RUBICON TRAIL

There are three trails at D. L. Bliss. The first one is a short self-guided nature trail to Balancing Rock (one-half mile). The second is a short trail to the lighthouse. The longest and most challenging is the Rubicon Trail (moderate), which follows the shoreline to Eagle Point campground on Emerald Bay (six miles). Fabulous views are found from the high bluffs that jet out over the deepest part of the lake that joins the shoreline. Boats of all types and sizes zoom by on the way to Emerald Bay. Many vintage postcards of the Steamer Tahoe show it passing Rubicon Point. Make sure to stop for other stunning views at the old lighthouse. Since the trail has a lot of ups and downs, it is a fairly tiring hike, so many people leave a car at both ends. Be sure to take plenty of water and a healthy lunch. No dogs are allowed on the park trails.
—*Rubicon Trail. Krista Shewmaker.*

EMERALD BAY STATE PARK

In 1969, Emerald Bay was designated a National Natural Landmark by the U.S. Department of Interior for its brilliant panorama of mountain-building processes and glacier carved granite. Few sites have been more photographed and painted. The Emerald Bay State Park encompasses 593 acres, which include the bay, Eagle Falls and Vikingsholm Castle. The bay itself is three miles long and one mile wide with Lake Tahoe's only island set in its center. There are high vantage lookout points at the northwest, west and southwest corners of the bay accessible by automobile. To get lake level views, you may walk the one-mile zigzag foot path from the northwest, arrive by pleasure craft or take one of the many tour-boat excursions offered. After heavy winter storms, the road often closes for a few days just north and south of the bay because of high avalanche danger.

—*Emerald Bay. Artist Missy Sandeman.*

VIKINGSHOLM

Vikingsholm was built for Lora Josephine Moore Knight, who purchased the property encompassing the head of Emerald Bay and Fannette Island in 1928 for $250,000. Two hundred workers were brought in to hand hew the timbers, carve the intricate designs and hand plane the wood for the interior walls. The ideas for the construction came from Scandinavian buildings dating as far back as the 11th century. Some sections of the home contain no nails or spikes. The interior of the home has paintings on some of the ceilings and walls and two intricately carved dragon beams. The six fireplaces are of Scandinavian design with unusual fireplace screens. A step into Vikingsholm is like a step back into medieval times and a chance to gain an appreciation of a unique style of architecture and the person who had it built.
—*Vikingsholm. Author.*

FANNETTE ISLAND

Fannette is the only island in Lake Tahoe—a sparsely timbered, brush covered upthrust of granite that rises 150 feet above the water. The stone structure on top was built for Mrs. Knight to use as a "Tea House" for entertaining her guests. A small fireplace in the corner and a large oak table and four oak chairs in the center of the 16-by-16 foot room gave it a very rustic appearance. Today, only the stone shell remains. From February 1 through June 15 the island is closed to all visitors, as during this period several pairs of Canada geese nest on the island. The virtual absence of predators makes this an ideal location for nesting. There may be as many as 100 geese on or near the island in the early spring. By late spring, it is not uncommon to see families of geese swimming along the shoreline near Vikingsholm.

—*Fannette Island. Ray Holstead.*

EMERALD BAY BOAT CAMP

The boat camp is located on the north side of Emerald Bay, approximately one-half mile east of Fannette Island, near the site of the old Emerald Bay Resort. The boat camp is normally open from Memorial Day through Labor Day, depending upon weather conditions. There are mooring buoys for the 20 campsites, and boaters can either sleep on board their boat, or camp in a designated site on shore. Each campsite has a table, storage locker and fire ring. Water is available in the campground, and there are chemical toilets. There are no showers. All campsites, with buoy, are available on a first-come, first-served basis. Visitors using the boat camp facilities must be registered and pay the required fees. There is a self-registration station on the shore near the dock. The dock is for loading and unloading only and there is a 15-day camping limit.

—*Emerald Bay Camp. Don and Jeanne Davis collection.*

Emerald Bay Camp, Lake Tahoe, Cal.

Putnam & Valentine Photo. Los Angeles. Cal.

UNDERWATER PARK

Emerald Bay was designated an underwater state park in 1994. Scuba divers have the opportunity to view and touch artifacts of an age long past. Emerald Bay State Underwater Park is the resting place for many boats, launches, and barges used in the lake before the turn of the century, during the heyday of Emerald Bay Resort and the construction of Vikingsholm. All artifacts are protected by state law and may not be taken or disturbed regardless of size or value. At the barge site on the southern shore, there are two historic barges in the same location as a dump site possibly used by Emerald Bay Resort and others from 1884 until 1953.

—*Emerald Bay, Lake Tahoe. Don and Jeanne Davis collection.*

HERMIT OF EMERALD BAY

Captain Richard Barter came to Emerald Bay in 1863 to caretake "The Cottage," a summer residence built by Ben Holladay Jr.—the first known private villa at the lake. Barter was an old English seaman and a heavy drinker who often said "Tahoe" was an Indian word for lager beer. For the first few years, life at Emerald Bay was uneventful, then Barter met with a series of misadventures. In January 1868, an avalanche missed him by about 10 feet, then, in 1870, Barter rowed up to Tahoe City to spend the day drinking in the Tahoe House Saloon. Two miles south of Sugar Pine Point, his boat capsized, tossing him into the icy waters. Though he made it home, his frozen toes become gangrenous, so he amputated them with a carving knife. During his confinement, Captain Dick built a 7-foot-long three-masted man-of-war.

—*An "almost frozen" Emerald Bay. Author.*

Captain Barter battled many other storms and decided to excavate a tomb on top of the bay's island for his final resting place. He surrounded it with a miniature Gothic chapel with a wooden cross on top of the steep roof. He told everyone that if his body was ever found lashed to his sailboat or washed up on shore, that he should be buried on Coquette Island (now called Fannette Island). He never tired of telling stories of avalanches and boating accidents to anyone who would listen, and when reporters came to interview him, he would pull out the bottle in the drawer stating proudly: "Them's my toes!" Barter's life ended in mid-October 1873, when waves broadsided his boat off Rubicon Point. He drowned in 1,400 feet of water and his body was never recovered. Legend has it that on chilly fall evenings, the ghost of Captain Richard Barter can be seen climbing slowly to the top of the island to find rest in his granite tomb.

—*Fannette Island. Krista Shewmaker.*

EAGLE FALLS, LAKE AND POINT

Lower Eagle Falls descend from the east side of the road to the back of Vikingsholm. Across the highway is the Eagle Falls Trail which ascends one-mile to Eagle Lake, passing spots where you can look down upon Emerald Bay and out to the Carson Range above Tahoe. Eagle Lake is a pleasant spot for picture taking, fishing and picnicking. Rockclimbers are drawn to the many granite cliffs in the area. After the lake, the trail enters Desolation Wilderness. Eagle Point Campground, part of Emerald Bay State Park, is located on the south point of the bay. It boasts 100 sites, many suitable for small RVs. Most of the camping areas are small and located among the pines, with picnic tables and barbeques. Bathrooms and hot showers are available. A trail runs from the campground along the shore to Vikingsholm, continuing on to the Rubicon Trail and D. L. Bliss State Park.

—*Emerald Bay. Debbie Arbogast-Haas.*

BAYVIEW CAMPGROUND AND TRAILHEAD

The Bayview Campground, operated by a USFS concession-aire, sits at the southwest end of Emerald Bay offering 10 spacious camp sites, available in summer on a first-come, first-served basis. Some sites are large enough for an RV. An easy one-mile hike south from the back of the campground leads to the upper side of Cascade Falls—another pleasant picnic spot—with nice views of Cascade Lake and Lake Tahoe. Heading in the opposite direction from the back of the campground is the Bayview Trailhead, leading into Desolation Wilderness and joining the Pacific Crest Trail. The campground has a tie-in for horses and equestrians use this as a gathering point for pack trips. Many fly fishing enthusiasts head to backcountry lakes from the Bayview and Eagles Falls trails.

—*Sunrise over Cascade Lake. Author.*

FLY FISHING DESOLATION LAKES

A main access point to Desolation Wilderness is the Eagle Lake Trail that heads in from Emerald Bay, or from its secondary entrance on the Bayview Trail just south of Emerald Bay. The main attraction here is Velma Lakes, about five miles in. These are stocked with put and grow rainbows which at maturity often reach 15 inches. They are particularly susceptible to damselfly imitations in July and terrestrials, especially grasshoppers, at any time. This is probably the most overused area in the Desolation and is not a place for solitude. Nonetheless, there are many secondary lakes that offer a place to get away from it all. For example, Granite Lake up the Bayview Trail a little over a mile has plenty of brookies. Due to the steepness of the trail, it is not often fished. A float tube is very useful in Granite and the other lakes of Desolation.

—*Velma stream. Jerry Yesavage.*

TAHOE AT A GLANCE

- Length: 22 miles / Width: 12 miles
- Elevation: 6,229 feet above sea level
- Shoreline: 71 miles, 42 in California and 29 in Nevada
- Inlets: 63 streams and 2 hot springs
- Outlet: Truckee River at Tahoe City is the only one
- Depth: Average is 989 feet, maximum is 1,645 feet
- Surface temperature: Ranges between 41 and 68 degrees fahrenheit
- Main body of the lake has never been known to freeze

The West Shore

- Average snowfall is 213 inches
- Winters are cold but not severe: January minimum 17-22°F , high 35-40°
- 70-120 frost-free days per year
- Winter sunshine is 60% of total possible hours

—*Aerial view of Lake Tahoe. Ann Riordan.*

DIRECTORY

- Places to Stay
- Vacation Rentals and Ski Leases
- Camping and Hut Reservations
- Dining
- Media with West Shore Coverage
- Things to See and Do
- Shopping
- Miscellaneous
- Road Conditions, Weather and Transportation
- Weddings
- Church Services
- Further information
- Beyond the West Shore

- On our Web Site

(S/O) = Summer Only
Means somewhere between
April through October, but always
July and August

(Y/R) = Year-round

Places to Stay

CHANEY HOUSE: Historic stone lakefront guest house.
Homewood 530-525-7333 www.chaneyhouse.com

COTTAGE INN B&B: Old Tahoe knotty pine cottages.
Sunnyside 530-581-4073 www.thecottageinn.com

GRANLIBAKKEN RESORT B&B: 160 room condominium resort. Tahoe
City (south) 800-543-3221 www.granlibakken.com

GRUBSTAKE LODGE: Rustic rooms and housekeeping units.
Homewood 530-525-5505

HOMESIDE MOTEL: Ranch style motel with knotty pine rooms.
Homewood 530-525-9990 www.homesidemotel.com

HOMEWOOD MARINA LODGE: Motel & cottages with kitchenettes.
Homewood 530-525-6728

MEEKS BAY RESORT: S/O Historic resort offering cabins, camping, and
marina w/great beach 530-525-6946 www.meeksbayresort.com

NORFOLK WOODS INN (B&B): Original old Tahoe inn.
Tahoma 530-525-5000 www.norfolkwoods.com

ROCKWOOD LODGE B&B: One of Tahoe's grand mansions.
Homewood 530-525-5273 www.rockwoodlodge.com

SUNNYSIDE RESORT LODGE: Charming lakefront lodge.
Sunnyside 530-583-7200 / 800-822-2SKI www.sunnysideresort.com

TAHOE CEDARS LODGE: (May-September) Vintage cabins in old Tahoe setting, private beach. Tahoma 530-525-7515

TAHOE LAKE COTTAGES: Cute, cozy, quiet, & clean.
Tahoma 530-525-4411 www.tahoelakecottages.com

TAHOMA LODGE: Quiet, comfortable cabins with kitchens.
Tahoma 530-525-7721 www.tahomalodge.com

TAHOMA MEADOWS B&B: Cozy red cabins with unique decor.
Tahoma 530-525-1553 www.tahomameadows.com

Vacation Rentals and Ski Leases

The following offer accommodations from small rustic cabins and condominiums to historic homes and glorious lakefront estates.

ACCOMMODATOR:530-525-0960 www.tahoeaccommodator.com

CHAMBERLANDS: 530-525-7263 www.tahoerentalgroup.com

EMERALD VACATIONS: 775-588-8955 www.emeraldvacations.com

HISTORIC LOG LODGE: (see Wells & Bennett below)

MITCHELL & ASSOCIATES: Homewood 530-525-3305, Tahoma 530-525-3300 and Rubicon 525-3310 www.realestatetahoe.com

ROCKY RIDGE: 800-222-5758 www.onealbrokers.com

TAHOE PARK REALTY: 530-583-6942 www.tahoeparkrealty.com

TAHOE REAL ESTATE GROUP: 800-655-7488 www.tahoerealestategroup.com

TAVERN PROPERTIES: 530-583-3704 www.onealbrokers.com

WEST LAKE PROPERTIES:530-583-0268 www.westlakeproperties.com

WELLS & BENNETT: 800-858-2463 www.tahoerentals.com

Camping and Hut Reservations

BAYVIEW CAMPGROUND: 530-544-0426
D.L.BLISS STATE PARK: 530-525-7277
EAGLE POINT CAMPGROUND: 530-541-3030
KASPIAN: 800-280-CAMP/2267
LUDLOW HUT: 530-426-3632 www.sierraclub.org
MEEKS BAY CAMPGROUND: 530-544-0426
SUGAR PINE POINT STATE PARK: Tahoe's only year-round campground, in Tahoma. 800-444-7275 or online www.parks.ca.gov
WILLIAM KENT: 800-280-CAMP/2267 www.reserveusa.com

Dining

ANGELA'S PIZZARIA: Traditional and gourmet Italian food. Tahoma 530-525-4771
BRIDGETENDER TAVERN: Patio dining overlooking the Truckee River. Full bar. Tahoe City South 530-583-3342

CHAMBERS LANDING: S/O Upscale restaurant and historic bar.
Homewood 530-525-7262 www.dinewine.com

FIRESIGN CAFE: Homestyle cooking in a cozy country atmosphere.
Sunnyside 530-583-0871

FOREST INN BLACK BEAR TAVERN: Restaurant and full bar
Sunnyside 530-583-8626

NORFOLK WOODS INN: Upscale dining, charming old Tahoe inn.
Tahoma 530-525-5000 www.norfolkwoods.com

OLD TAHOE CAFE: Homey, family oriented establishment. Homewood
530-525-5437

STONY RIDGE CAFE: Creative menu, fresh ingredients, espresso
Tahoma 530-525-0905 www.stonyridgecafe.com

SUNNYSIDE RESORT: Old Tahoe charm with casual elegance, on the
lake. Sunnyside 530-583-7200 www.sunnysideresort.com

SWISS LAKEWOOD: Upscale historic restaurant offering European style
cuisine. Homewood 530-525-5211

TAHOE HOUSE: Swiss and California cuisine. European style bakery. Tahoe City South 530-583-1377

WEST SHORE CAFE: S/O (soon to be Y/R) Elegant outdoor cafe dining on the lake. Homewood 530-525-5200 www.westshorecafe.com

Media with West Shore Coverage

TAHOE QUARTERLY: www.tahoequarterly.com

NORTH TAHOE/TRUCKEE THIS WEEK: www.tahoethisweek.com

TAHOE WORLD: www.tahoe.com

Things to Do and See

ALPINE MEADOWS SKI AREA: European-style resort w/2,000 acres 530-583-4232 www.skialpine.com

ARTOUR: August. Artists open studios www.tahoeartists.com

BIKE TRAIL: S/O 11 miles along the West Shore—Tahoe City to Meeks Bay. Also goes west to Squaw Valley and east to Dollar Point.

CASCADE STABLES: S/O Horseback trips up Meeks Bay Trail into Desolation Wilderness. 530-541-2055

CLASSIC CRUISES: S/O Charter boat cruises aboard a 1936 sedan cruiser (up to six passengers). 530-525-4055

CYCLEPATHS MOUNTAIN BIKE ADVENTURES: S/O For all levels Sunnyside 530-581-1171 or 800-780-BIKE www.cyclepaths.com

FANNY BRIDGE BIKE AND RAFT: S/O Rental reservations recommended. Tahoe City South 530-581-0123

EHRMAN MANSION: Grounds open Y/R, interior visits S/O. Sugar Pine Point State Park, Tahoma 530-525-7982

FIREWORKS: July 5th, organized by West Shore Café Homewood 530-525-5200 www.westshorecafe.com

FLY FISHING DESOLATION WILDERNESS: Book and Web site www.stanford.edu/people/yesavage/Desolation.html

GATEKEEPER'S CABIN MUSEUM: S/O Discover the area's history Tahoe City South 530-583-1762 www.tahoecountry.com/nlths

GRANLIBAKKEN RESORT: Ski, sled, bike, tennis Tahoe City South 530-581-7533 www.granlibakken.com

HIGH SIERRA WATER SKI SCHOOL: S/O For all ages.
530-583-7417 and Homewood Marina 530-525-1214

HOMEWOOD HARDWARE: X- country ski rentals. Homewood 530-525-6367 www.homewoodhardware.com

HOMEWOOD HIGH & DRY MARINA: S/O Full service marina
Homewood 530-525-5966

HOMEWOOD MOUNTAIN RESORT: Full service ski resort with 1,260 acres. Facilities are available to rent in summer for events and weddings. Homewood 530-525-2992 www.skihomewood.com

INSIDE OUT FITNESS: Health Club Tahoe City South 530-581-5541

JOHNSON'S TACKLE & GUIDE: Instructional fly fishing guide
Tahoma 530-525-6575 www.flyfishingtahoe.com

KINGFISH GUIDE SERVICE: Y/R Fishing trips; S/O Tours to Emerald Bay. Homewood 530-525-5360

LAKE TAHOE MARATHON: Annually in October around entire lake.
www.laketahoemarathon.com

LAKE TAHOE SUMMER MUSIC FESTIVAL: S/O Classical and jazz, in and outdoors 530-583-3101 www.tahoemusic.org

MARIE SLUCHAK COMMUNITY PARK: July and August: Free movies Saturday evenings, Sunday church services, Christmas gala first Saturday in December 530-525-6169

MARION STEINBACH INDIAN BASKET MUSEUM: S/O Tahoe City South 530-583-1762 www.tahoecountry.com/nlths

MEEKS BAY MARINA: S/0 530-525-5588 www.meeksbayresort.com

MEEKS BAY PANCAKE BREAKFAST: Independance Day weekend at the Meeks Bay Fire Station 530-525-7548

OBEXER'S MARINA: S/0 Moorings, deepwater ramp, gas, supplies, repairs. Homewood 530-525-7962

PARKS AND RECREATION PROGRAMS: Y/R Periodic programs offered along the West Shore 530-583-3796

RALPH'S SAILBOAT: S/O Children's ski school, Ski/Sail National Championships. Homewood 530-525-SAIL

RIDE THE RUBICON: S/O ATV /Hummer rides up the McKinney-Rubicon Trail. 530-577-2940 www.laketahoeadventure.com

SNOWFEST: Annual North Shore winter festival late February-early April with some West Shore events. 775-832-7625 www.snowfest.com

TAHOE STREET ARTS FESTIVAL: S/O Homewood 530-583-5605

TAHOE GEAR: Outdoor recreation specialists skiing and biking. Homewood 530-525-5233 www.homewoodtahoegear.com

TENNIS COURTS: S/O Sugar Pine Point State Park, Ehrman Mansion Complex 530-525-7982; Ward Park Sunnyside (first-come, first-served at both)

VIKINGSHOLM: Emerald Bay State Park Mansion and Visitor's Center S/O 530-525-7232

WILDFLOWER WALKS: Offered at various locations such as Meeks Bay and Emerald Bay. Keep watch on our calendar www.tahoecountry.com

WINTER STATE PARK PROGRAMS: Contact Sierra District Office after October 1 for program 530-525-3345

WOODEN BOAT WEEK: In August. Some West Shore venues
Contact: Tahoe Yacht Club 530-581-4700 www.tahoeyc.com

Shopping

ALPACA PETES: Import shop. Meeks Bay 530-525-5328
www.alpacapetes.com
CHATEAU CADEAU: Home furnishings, decorating.
Tahoe City South 530-583-5101 www.chateaucadeau.com
FARMER'S MARKET: Homewood, Sundays in July and August
GIRASOLE: Antiques, gifts and decorating. Tahoe City South
530-581-4255
LISA'S ORGANICS: Weekly home delivery of your choice of organic
foods & produce. 530-582-2280 www.lisasorganics.com
MEEKS BAY MARKET: S/O
NEW MOON: Natural health food store. Tahoe City South
530-583-7426

PDQ OBEXER'S COUNTRY MARKET Homewood: Groceries, deli, espresso, liquor. 530-525-1300; PDQ TAHOMA MARKET AND DELI Tahoma: Groceries, deli, liquor, video rental. 530-525-7411

PORTER'S OUTLET: Ski and sport equipment, accessories, rentals. Tahoe City South 530-583-0293

SUNNYSIDE MARKET: Full-service market with groceries, deli, video rentals, fax service, and souvenirs. Sunnyside 530-583-7626

TAHOE HOUSE BAKERY: European style bakery and espresso bar. Tahoe City South 530-583-1377 www.tahoehouse.com

TAHOE TREE COMPANY: Nursery, gifts, espresso and snack bar. Tahoe City South 530-583-3911 www.tahoetree.com

Miscellaneous

BEAR LEAGUE: 530-525-7297 www.savebears.org

DESOLATION WILDERNESS: 530-573-2600

CALIFORNIA STATE PARKS–SIERRA DISTRICT:
530-525-7232 http://ceres.ca.gov/sierradsp/

LAKE TAHOE DATA CLEARINGHOUSE: http://tahoe.usgs.gov/

LEAGUE TO SAVE LAKE TAHOE: 530-584-1660

www.keeptahoeblue.org

OLYMPIC TRAILS RECONSTRUCTION PROJECT:

www.olympictrails.org

PACIFIC CREST TRAIL: 916-349-2109 www.pcta.org

SNO-PARK PERMIT FOR KASPIAN RECREATION AREA: Tahoe National Forest 530-587-3558 www.r5.fs.fed.us/tahoe/

TAHOE MARITIME MUSEUM: 530-583-5028

www.tahoemaritimemuseum.org

TAHOE RIM TRAIL 775-588-0686 www.tahoerimtrail.org

U.S.FOREST SERVICE—LAKE TAHOE BASIN MANAGEMENT UNIT: 530-573-2600 www.r5.fs.fed.us/ltbmu/

Road Conditions, Weather and Transportation

AIRPORTS: Reno/Tahoe in Reno (one hour from West Shore)775-328-6400 www. renotahoeairport.com; Truckee Airport small craft only, 530-

587-4119; South Lake Tahoe 530-541-4082 www.laketahoeairport.com

BUS: Greyhound stops in Truckee and South Lake Tahoe
www.greyhound.com

GAS: Cut-Rite in Tahoma is the West Shore's only gas station (between
Tahoe City and South Lake Tahoe) 530-525-7704

RAILWAY: Amtrak stops daily in Truckee 800-872-7245
www.amtrak.com

RENTAL CARS: Contact Reno/Tahoe airport (above); A and A Truckee
Tahoe Rental will meet you in Truckee at the airport, bus, or train 530-
582-8282

ROAD CONDITIONS: Keep this number handy. CALTRANS 800-427-
7623 (punch in Highway # for updated report)

ROAD MAPS: www.mapquest.com

TAXIS: Tahoe Truckee Taxi serves the West Shore 530-583-8294

SHUTTLES: Cyclepaths shuttle service to/from airport in Reno and other
needs for groups 530-581-1171 www.cyclepaths.com

TART (Tahoe City Regional Transit): Runs from Meeks Bay to Incline Village and Truckee 530-550-1212

TAHOE CITY TROLLEY: Bus runs as overflow to TART during summer

TOPO MAPS: http://maps.nationalgeographic.com/topo/

TOWING COMPANY: AAA 800-222-4357

WEATHER: www.weather.com

WEBCAM-SUGAR PINE POINT STATE PARK: http://ceres.ca.gov/sierradsp/

Weddings

Contact: Forest Inn Black Bear Tavern, Chamber's Landing, Granlibakken Resort, Homewood Mountain Resort, Meeks Bay Resort, Norfolk Woods Inn, Sugar Pine Point State Park, Sunnyside Resort, Tahoe Lake Cottages and West Shore Cafe.

Church Services

CORPUS CHRISTI CATHOLIC CHURCH, Tahoe City South 530-583-4409

NON-DENOMINATIONAL: Outdoor services Sundays 9 a.m. July-August at Marie Sluchak Community Park, Tahoma 530-525-6169

SAINT NICHOLAS EPISCOPAL: Tahoe City South 530-583-4713

Further Information

TAHOE COUNTRY Web Site www.tahoecountry.com

WEST SHORE ASSOCIATION Post Office Box 844, Homewood, CA 96141 530-584-1248

Beyond the West Shore

(Chambers of Commerce and Visitors Bureaus)

ALPINE COUNTY 530-694-2475 www.alpinecounty.com

AUBURN AREA 530-885-5616 www.auburnchamber.net

CARSON CITY 775-882-1565 www.carsoncitychamber.com

CARSON VALLEY 775-782-8144 www.carsonvalleynv.org

INCLINE-CRYSTAL BAY 775-831-4440 www.laketahoechamber.com

EL DORADO COUNTY 530-621-5885 www.eldoradocounty.org

LAKE TAHOE VISITORS AUTHORITY www.virtualtahoe.com

NEVADA CITY 530-265-2692 www.ncgold.com
NORTH LAKE TAHOE RESORT ASSOCIATION 530-583-3494
www.tahoefun.org
RENO-SPARKS 775-686-3030 www.reno-sparkschamber.org
SOUTH LAKE TAHOE 530-541-5255 www.tahoeinfo.org
TAHOE-DOUGLAS (STATELINE) 775-588-4591 www.tahoechamber.org
TRUCKEE 530-587-2757 www.truckee.com
VIRGINIA CITY 775-847-0311 www.virginiacity-nv.com

On Our Web Site

WWW.TAHOECOUNTRY.COM
- Calendar of events, virtual tours, business directory and related links
- A clearinghouse for Lake Tahoe history and vintage postcard exhibits
- A place to ask questions or submit stories and photos to share
- Flora and fauna, home and garden and lots of local flavor
- Send virtual greeting cards of photos, art and vintage postcards
- Online store of regional products from the High Sierra

BIBLIOGRAPHY

There have been many books written about the Lake Tahoe region, all notable for filling particular niches. The following are some favorites for their outstanding contributions to recording Lake Tahoe history—all of which were utilized in the writing of *Tahoe's Magical West Shore*:

Lake Tahoe Lake of the Sky by George Wharton James
Nevada Publications
Meeks Bay Memories by Carol Van Etten.
Sierra Maritime Publications
Saga of Lake Tahoe Volumes I & II by Edward B. Scott
Sierra-Tahoe Publishing Co.
Tahoe: from Timber Barons to Ecologists by Douglas H. Strong
University of Nebraska Press
The Tahoe Sierra by Jeffrey P. Schaffer
Wilderness Press

A BIG THANKS TO ALL

Jill

ACKNOWLEDGMENTS

David Antonucci
Debbie Arbogast-Haas
Brook Austin
Betty Barsamian
Paul Bartmettler
Bob Beede
Justin Beede
Miriam Biro
Bill Briner
Kim Broyles
Scott Brunn
Yvonna Butz
Douglas Byrne
Cathy Carew

Bill Clausen
Pat Davi
Mike Davies
Don and Jeanne Davis
Roy E. Dryer III
Greg Forsyth
Danielle Hansen
Pauline Harder
Ray and Cathy Holstead
Sara Hurley
Don Lane
Steve Lapkin
Bill Lindeman
De Macrae

Liz McMillan
Roz and John Mitchell
Evelyn Nored
Sarah Obexer
Ron Patterson
Tara Pielaet
Melinda Plumbridge
Bruce Rettig
Ann Riordan
Missy Sandeman
Krista Shewmaker
Mona Schulte
Ralph Silverman
Dick Singer
Tom Singer
Marie Sluchak

Mike Stuckey
Randi Urdahl
Carol Van Etten
Layne Van Noy
Jerry Yesavage
Deby Zwierlein-Carter

* * * * *

California State Parks Sierra District
Nevada State Museum
North Lake Tahoe Historical Society
Pacific Crest Trail Association
Tahoe City Public Utility District
Tahoe Rim Trail Association
United States Forest Service—Lake
Tahoe Basin Management Unit

Cover Credits

Chambers Bar. Artist Bill Clausen.
Squirrel. Author's collection.
Indian Women. Author's collection.
Girls at Lakeside. Debbie Arbogast-Haas.
Wooden Boat. Artist Roy E. Dryer III.
Black Bear. Scott Brunn.
Winter Trees. Artist Missy Sandeman.
Quail Lake in the Fall. Artist Melinda Plumbridge.
Historic Log Lodge. Ron Patterson.
Emerald Bay Circle. Artist Liz McMillan.
Cover collage and map design: Betty Barsamian

INDEX

ABOUT THE AUTHOR

Jill Beede first discovered Lake Tahoe as a child—coming to the West Shore on family vacations from the San Francisco Bay Area. After college, she moved to Europe to complete post-graduate studies and work in the travel industry. Jill returned to California to teach, and later, after spending another year abroad as a Fulbright Exchange Teacher in the Jura mountains of France, she decided to make Lake Tahoe her home. Jill has written educational materials, was a contributing editor to *France Today* magazine for four years and editor of the West Shore's *Tahoma Tattler* from 1991 to 1999. In 1996, she began promoting the Lake Tahoe region with her webzine of travel and culture, *TahoeCountry.com*, and after visitors from around the globe continued to request printed information about Lake Tahoe, Jill decided to develop a series of regional guidebooks. *Tahoe's Magical West Shore*, the first, is a celebration of her love for the area that first introduced her to the High Sierra.